MURDER HORNETS

by Jaclyn Jaycox

PEBBLE
a capstone imprint

Published by Pebble, an imprint of Capstone
1710 Roe Crest Drive, North Mankato, Minnesota 56003
capstonepub.com

Library of Congress Cataloging-in-Publication Data is available on the Library of Congress website.

ISBN: 9781666342772 (hardcover)
ISBN: 9781666342819 (paperback)
ISBN: 9781666342857 (ebook PDF)

Summary: Young readers learn all about murder hornets, including where they live, their bodies, and what they do.

Image Credits
Alamy: Nature Picture Library, 17, Nobuo Matsumura, 20; Capstone Press, 6; Getty Images: Bruno Uehara, 13, feathercollector, Cover, kojihirano, 12, kororokerokero, 11, 23, wenbin, 26, yamasan, 7; Minden Pictures: Satoshi Kuribayashi, 5; Shutterstock: 5D2, 27, CatherineLProd, 21, Contrail, 14, Ken Kojima, 28, Naoto Shinkai, 1, 9, NitayaPhet, 24, Purino, 18, Tatiana. Sidorova, 8

Editorial Credits
Editor: Abby Huff; Designer: Dina Her; Media Researchers: Jo Miller and Pam Mitsakos; Production Specialist: Tori Abraham

All internet sites appearing in back matter were available and accurate when this book was sent to press.

Table of Contents

Words in **bold** are in the glossary.

Amazing Murder Hornets

Buzz! A big orange and brown **insect** flies by. What could it be? A murder hornet! These insects are actually Asian giant hornets. They can wipe out entire hives of honeybees. Because of this, they have been nicknamed murder hornets.

There are more than 20 kinds of hornets. Murder hornets are the largest in the world.

Where in the World

Murder hornets live in Japan and across East Asia. They live in low mountains. They are found in forests too. They prefer areas that get warm and cool. But they also live in places that stay warm and wet all the time.

Murder Hornets Range Map

North America

Europe

Asia

Pacific Ocean

Atlantic Ocean

Pacific Ocean

Africa

South America

Indian Ocean

Australia

Range

N
W E
S

Southern Ocean

Antarctica

workers

Murder hornets live in groups called colonies. Each colony has a special female. She is the queen. She is the only one that lays eggs. Other hornets are called workers.

A nest built between rocks

Murder hornets make nests. They often make them in the ground. They dig out a spot. Or they use tunnels left by animals. Some build nests higher up. They build in tree trunks. They also use other small spaces above ground.

The nest is made of comb. Hornets chew up bark. Then they spit it out. The mix dries to make comb.

Murder Hornet Bodies

What's the easiest way to spot a murder hornet? By its huge size! Queens are the biggest. They grow more than 2 inches (5 centimeters) long. That's five times larger than a honeybee!

Worker hornets are smaller than the queen. They are about 1.5 inches (3.8 cm) long.

Like all insects, a murder hornet's body has three sections. It has a head, **thorax**, and **abdomen**.

The head is yellow or orange. It has two feelers called **antennae**. They are used to smell, hear, and touch.

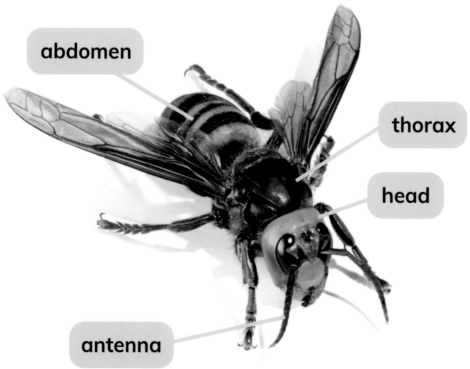

abdomen

thorax

head

antenna

Murder hornets have big mouthparts. They bite food. The hornets also have a special black tooth. It's used for digging.

stinger

The thorax is the middle part of the body. Six legs grow out of it. Two pairs of large wings are also found here.

The abdomen is the last body part. It has orange and brown stripes. Only females have stingers. The stinger is about as long as a pencil eraser! **Venom** flows out of it when hornets sting. They can sting over and over. Many stings can be deadly!

On the Menu

Day is over. Night is here. A group of murder hornets fly near a beehive. They spot their **prey**. It's time to attack!

The hornets tear up the bees with their mouthparts. They go into the hive. They find the bee **larvae**. They chew the larvae into a paste. The hornets fly back to their nest. They feed the paste to their young.

Murder hornets attack a beehive.

Murder hornet larvae eat bee larvae. The adult hornets attack hives to get the food. A hornet can kill as many as 40 honeybees in one minute.

Adult murder hornets mainly eat other insects. They hunt bees, wasps, and other hornets. But they will eat fruit and tree sap too.

Life of a Murder Hornet

Murder hornets **mate** in the fall. A male mates with a queen. The male dies soon after. The queen finds a place to spend the winter. She **hibernates** under tree bark or in the ground. She wakes in the spring.

Queens come out of the ground in spring.

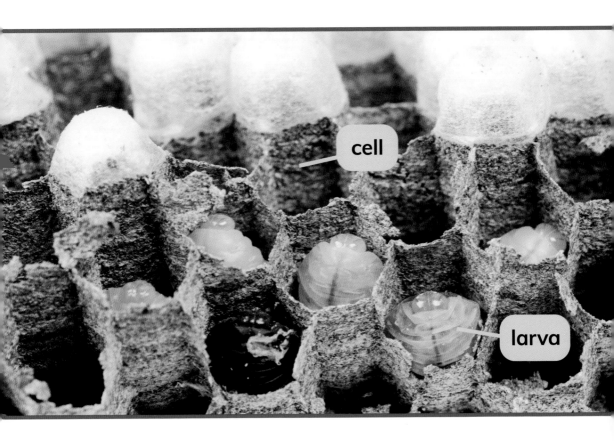

cell

larva

The queen makes a nest alone. She lays her first eggs. There are up to 40. Each one has its own spot in the nest called a cell. The eggs hatch larvae after about a week.

The queen takes care of the larvae. She brings them food. They grow. After two weeks, the young cover their cells with silk. They keep growing for about two more weeks. When they come out, they are adults.

The new adult hornets are ready to work! The queen's only job now is to lay more eggs. The workers keep building the nest. They go out to find food. They take care of new larvae.

Workers find food, such as sap.

A nest filled with many young hornets

By the end of summer, the queen has laid close to 1,000 eggs. Some of the last eggs will hatch new queens. The old queen will die before winter comes.

In the fall, the new queens and males leave the nest. They mate. The males die. The queens find places to hibernate. The life cycle begins again.

Dangers to Murder Hornets

Murder hornets don't have **predators**.
Humans are their biggest danger.
In some areas, people eat them.
People are also cutting down forests.
Murder hornets are losing their homes.

honeybees

Some honeybees have learned to fight back. When a murder hornet enters the hive, bees rush over. They form a ball around the hornet. They move back and forth quickly. This creates heat. The hornet gets too hot and dies.

Murder hornets can be harmful in new places. Bees in other places don't know how to fight back. Many could be killed.

A few murder hornets were found in the U.S. in 2019. Scientists think they may have come on ships bringing goods from Asia. People are working hard to keep the hornets from spreading.

Fast Facts

Name: murder hornet or Asian giant hornet

Habitat: low mountains, forests

Where in the World: Japan, East Asia

Food: bee larvae, bees, wasps, hornets, fruit, tree sap

Predators: humans

Life Span: workers up to 1 month and queens up to 1 year

Glossary

abdomen (AB-duh-muhn)—the back section of an insect's body

antenna (an-TEH-nuh)—a body part that sticks out from an insect's head, used to touch, hear, and smell

hibernate (HI-ber-neyt)—to spend winter in a deep sleep

insect (IN-sekt)—a small animal with a hard outer shell, six legs, three body sections, and two antennae

larva (LAR-vuh)—an insect at the stage of its life cycle between an egg and an adult

mate (MEYT)—to join together to produce young

predator (PREH-duh-tur)—an animal that hunts other animals for food

prey (PRAY)—an animal hunted by another animal for food

thorax (THOR-aks)—the middle section of an insect's body where wings and legs are attached

venom (VEN-uhm)—a poison made by an animal

Read More

Gray, Susan H. *Murder Hornets Invade Honeybee Colonies*. Ann Arbor, MI: Cherry Lake Publishing Group, 2022.

Hansen, Grace. *Asian Giant Hornet*. Minneapolis: Abdo Kids, 2021.

Katz, Susan B. *Is It a Honeybee or a Wasp?* North Mankato, MN: Pebble, 2022.

Internet Sites

Kiddle: Hornet Facts for Kids
kids.kiddle.co/hornet

Newsround: What's the Difference between Wasps, Bees and Hornets?
bbc.co.uk/newsround/45194754

SoftSchools: Asian Giant Hornet Facts
softschools.com/facts/animals/asian_giant_hornet_facts/2311/

Index

About the Author

Jaclyn Jaycox is a children's book author and editor. She lives in southern Minnesota with her husband, two kids, and a spunky goldendoodle.